DOTTY WELDON

PINTASTIC MARKETING

The Ultimate Guide to the Power of Pinterest, Learn
Useful Methods and Techniques on How You Can Build
and Market Your Business Using Pinterest

Descrierea CIP a Bibliotecii Naţionale a României
DOTTY WELDON
   PINTASTIC MARKETING. The Ultimate Guide to the Power of Pinterest, Learn Useful Methods and Techniques on How You Can Build and Market Your Business Using Pinterest / Dotty Weldon – Bucharest: Editura My Ebook, 2021
   ISBN

DOTTY WELDON

PINTASTIC MARKETING

The Ultimate Guide to the Power of Pinterest, Learn Useful Methods and Techniques on How You Can Build and Market Your Business Using Pinterest

My Ebook Publishing House
Bucharest, 2021

CONTENTS

Contents

WHY IS PINTEREST SO POWERFUL?

If you're a marketer and you're not on Pinterest, then you're missing out on one of the biggest and the most flexible/powerful platforms out there. Pinterest may not be quite as big as Facebook in terms of pure users but it's actually not as far behind as you might think. What's more, it has a ton of unique features that present excellent opportunities for the savvy marketer.

The main problem that brands seem to have when it comes to Pinterest is that they don't see how they can get it to relate to them. Pinterest is very visual and creative, it's made up of images that people pin to their 'boards' and that others can then comment on or 're-pin'. Thus it *clearly* lends itself to companies that have an artistic, trendy, stylish or visual side. But how can this possibly be useful for a company that sells life insurance? Or for a blogger who is promoting the 'work online' lifestyle?

And seeing as Facebook and Twitter are so much bigger, does it really matter?

Well the first thing you should get out of your head is the idea that Pinterest isn't that big. In fact, Pinterest currently has 100 million users which is really pretty massive – and a subset of the market that you just can't ignore. Also interesting is that 85% of those 100 million users are female. This is quite unique for any social network and provides you with a great way to reach a female audience – something that a lot of blogs and brands could stand to do a little more effectively. 42% of all adult women in the US use Pinterest which is massive – and actually 13% of males do which is still rather significant.

And while Pinterest has a ton of users, it also has the advantage of being a platform that visitors can enjoy *without* signing up. That means that your potential reach is in fact much larger than you might at first have thought.

Pinterest is also one of the fastest growing platforms and is expected to acquire another 47.5 million users in 2015.

So you *need* to be on Pinterest and this is especially true once you realise that there are *plenty* of ways you can succeed on the platform even if your niche isn't terribly creative or visual. Over the course of this book we'll look at some more creative and imaginative approaches that you can take to your

Pinterest marketing and we'll see how many other brands have managed to take the network by storm.

Better yet, you'll find that Pinterest is actually one of the easiest social networks to manage and maintain. The amount of time and money you'll invest here is miniscule, and especially when compared with the amount you stand to gain. This is a very high ROI and it demands your attention!

With that in mind, this book is going to act as your comprehensive guide to mastering Pinterest. By the end, you'll know everything you need to know to get set up and to start building a massive audience. What's more, we'll go over some advanced strategies and techniques you can employ to get one step ahead of the competition and to accelerate your growth trajectory. You'll be armed with unrivalled knowledge of the platform and you'll be poised and ready to become a real force to be reckoned with on the platform.

Specifically, you will learn:

- How Pinterest works and what makes it different from other platforms
- How to get started with your own Pinterest boards
- How the top brands on Pinterest are making use of the platform

- How to save time using plugins and other tools

- How to market your Pinterest board through other forms of social media, email and more

- How to create stunning content that is destined to succeed on Pinterest

- Growth hack techniques for gaining more users more quickly

- What to expect from Pinterest moving forward

PINTEREST BASICS

Hopefully that's convinced you that you should start paying more attention to Pinterest. The next question then is... how?

How does Pinterest work? What does it offer that's different from other social networks? And how do you go about getting set up?

Essentially, Pinterest works by allowing you to create 'mood boards'. Anyone who has done an art course will be familiar with this term. For everyone else, a mood board is essentially a collage made up of images and other materials that you've found on the web. This lets you collect images and notes from anywhere online and to categorize them in one spot as a 'board'. These boards can then be shared by other users and brands and you can follow either individual boards or users if you'd like to see more that they've created or collected.

To find images to pin to your boards, you can either browse other boards and then 're- pin' the content you like, you can save images from the web and use social sharing buttons, or you can create your own content to upload to the site. You can use the in- built search tools in Pinterest to search for users, for boards or for specific items. If you want to see images of 'futuristic fonts' for instance, then you can search for that string and you'll be provided with a ton of images that other people and brands have pinned. Images have hashtags on them which describe their content and this then helps you when you're searching for more content.

The key difference that Pinterest has when compared to something like Facebook then, is that the social aspect is actually not at the forefront. You can keep the boards you create as 'private' if you like and this then means that no one else will see them. This means you can use it simply to collect ideas for your own projects or for your general inspiration – and CEO Ben Silbermann actually describes the tool as a 'catalogue of ideas' rather than a social network. His hope is that it can be used to inspire to people to, in his words, 'go do that thing'.

Once you're following a number of boards and users, you'll also be able to see pins that your contacts have pinned or commented on. You'll also images based on similar pins you have uploaded. This creates a 'homefeed' of sorts that you can browse just to find images you might find interesting or inspiring, or to see what your friends are up to.

Not sure what you want to search for? You can also use a button along the top in order to browse popular pins in specific categories – whether that's fashion, wedding, sports, art, architecture or pets.

Like any social network, Pinterest also offers a plethora of social elements. Other than using it to browse different users' content and edit it, it can also allow you to post comments on the pins you like (or don't like!), or to re-pin the content you enjoy and thereby share it with your own network. It's also possible to invite people to edit your boards and to set them up to be informed every time you add a new pin to it. This is a great feature for working on collaborative projects for instance and the boards are known as 'group boards'.

There are many more features to Pinterest than this. In fact, even if you have been using Pinterest for a while there's a very good chance that you won't have seen everything it has to offer and that you won't know all the different things you can do with the platform. Further in this book, we'll be looking at some of those more advanced features in more detail and seeing how you can utilize them for marketing benefits.

POPULAR USES FOR PINTEREST

So then, what do most people use Pinterest for?

As mentioned, Pinterest essentially revolves around mood boards which are designed to provide inspiration or to collect ideas.

One of the most popular types of boards that users will create for this purpose as an example are 'wedding boards'. When an engaged couple begin planning their wedding, they will often start by creating a Pinterest board and then looking for inspiration. They'll then look at boards created by other users and search for ideas for wedding dresses, for wedding locations, for table decorations, for cakes, for suits etc. (or they may create separate boards for each of those things).

Either way, they can then find new ideas and inspiration to guide their decisions and they can put all of these ideas into one spot to serve as a reference. Because you can work on boards collaboratively, the bride and groom can both go about looking for different ideas together at the same time and add them to the board so they can both see them. They can also add their own notes to read later, etc.

If you have photos on your computer of a wedding you've been to and really enjoyed meanwhile, you can upload photos from there. Or you can write notes and draw sketches and upload those as pins.

You can also show other people those same ideas to see what your maid of honor thinks of your ideas so far for example, or you can let other users see your board and get inspiration from you that way.

There are many other common ways that Pinterest gets used. Here are just a few:

- Collecting images that you find appealing/inspiring
- Collating ideas and inspiration for a new web design/app UI
- Getting ideas for interior design
- Browsing products and 'window shopping'
- Putting together inspirational images to get you into the gym (moves, 'goal physiques' etc.)
- Staying updated with your favorite brand in a more visual manner

- Looking at fashion and outfit ideas for clothes
- Researching tattoo ideas
- And much more

Of course what *we're* really interested in though, using Pinterest as a marketing tool…

MARKETING WITH PINTEREST

Now you know the basics of how Pinterest works, it's time to look at how this can be used by marketers and why Pinterest is such a powerful tool beyond just being a big platform to reach a large audience.

What features in particular make Pinterest a good choice for your business? How do you go about using it to promote your website or company?

As mentioned, a lot of people will use Pinterest primarily for researching ideas and getting inspiration. If they enjoy interior design, graphic design, fashion or fitness, they'll likely have lots of boards relating to that topic. What's more, they'll probably be following some other boards created by big brands in those areas.

As a brand, your objective is to be 'one of those brands' that people follow and to use this as a prime opportunity to show off your products, your services and your website so that you get more visitors and more business.

This is particularly easy if you should happen to work in one of the industries that is particularly popular on Instagram. If you create wedding decorations for instance, then all you need to do is to create a board dedicated to these and then let people pin the items they find there or just browse your site for ideas. The more people you can get to follow you, the more people will see your products, will be exposed to your brand and will likely buy your items. This ultimately means you can get a lot of traffic and engagement from a well thought-out Pinterest board.

What will help here is the ability to easily add links to your website and specific articles and blog posts. If you choose to 'Pin From the Web', you can then type in an URL and select an image from that website to go along with it. Under the pin, it will then say 'Pinned from' and you can click that to follow through to the blog post or article where it was originally posted. This means that people can follow your boards to stay up-to-date with your new articles and blog posts if they want as well, which they may choose to do if Pinterest is their preferred platform.

Beyond the basic features, there are also some more advanced options and tools on Pinterest that are going to be especially useful for marketers.

One example is 'Article Rich Pins'. These have been around since September 2013 and they basically take the central concept of posting links to blogs and articles and build on it. These allow you to share links as you already could but the additional advantage is that you can add extra information about the article – such as the title, the site name, the description and the author. This makes your blog and article links considerably more appealing and it encourages people to sign up automatically.

Article rich pins are actually just *one* of the advance types of 'rich pins' available for marketers and we'll be looking at more in further detail later in this book.

Another relatively new and big feature of Pinterest that is *particularly* interesting for marketers is the 'buyable pins' tool. This was introduced relatively recently (June 2015) so not every marketer is making full use of it.

As the name suggests, buyable pins are pins showing products that are for sale. So if you should be browsing the site and see an item of clothing, a desktop accessory, or maybe a piece of furniture that you like, then you can simply click to buy it. In the iPad and iPhone apps, the 'Pin It' button is now accompanied by a 'Buy It' button that lets users immediately buy the products they're interested in. By the end of the very first month, there were already 2 million of these pins on the site.

Pinterest has long been popular as a tool for 'window shopping'. When users are looking through other brand boards because they're looking for ideas for wedding decorations, things to wear or things to decorate their house with, they will often then follow the links to buy the products, or later look up the product.

But now with buyable pins, they can buy the product straight through Pinterest itself. This turns your Pinterest board into an ecommerce store, essentially meaning that anything on your site can now be easily bought. If you imagine that someone has taken a lot of time amassing a selection of items they find inspiring for their wedding, this means they can now eventually whittle that selection down just to the things they want and click 'buy'. This creates the barrier to sale and makes it a much thinner line between 'discovery' and sale. It's very simple and easy and it's a very tempting new option for businesses.

Finally, Pinterest also provides a large amount of analytics data. To get access to this you'll need to convert your personal account to a 'business account' and at the same time, you'll need to verify your account. From there, you'll then be able to see what pins are getting pinned from your website or blog. This in turn lets you see which content is really performing well and engaging your audience.

That's right, if you want to take full advantage of the analytics features on Pinterest, then you need to upgrade to a business account. And there are other advantages of making this switch too.

Can you promote your blog or business with a personal account? Of course you can: to an extent. But there are some considerable advantages of making the switch.

For starters, Pinterest actually requires you to make your Pinterest account a business one if you intend on using it to profit. While it's unlikely they'll clamp down on you for posting links to your website, you should switch if you want to tow the official line.

Their statement on the matter is:

"If you're using Pinterest as part of how you make a living, whether by driving traffic to a blog that makes you some money or to build your personal brand to find customers for

your products or services, you should sign up for a business account and agree to our Business Terms of Service."

From here, you'll then be able to display your company or brand name as the title of your Pinterest profile instead of your first and last name, you'll be able to get insider tips and strategies from Pinterest (they provide a lot of free educational materials) and you'll be able to verify your website. As mentioned, it's this latter step that enables you to see which of your photos and images are getting shared on Pinterest, getting repined and getting commented on.

Verifying your URL also has another benefit – it adds your hyperlink to the top of your profile. This now means that anyone who discovers your Pinterest account will now be able to quickly discover your website as well and that means more traffic, more ad clicks, more sales etc.

Business accounts are also allowed to host contests through their Pinterest, which is something we'll be looking at more further on in this book.

THE PINTEREST INTERFACE

When you first log into Pinterest, it can be a little overwhelming and daunting. The site looks very different to something like Twitter or Facebook and at first, the navigation might not seem that intuitive. How do you find the boards you like the looks of? How do you find your way around?

When you're first signed up and logged in, you'll be greeted by your home-feed which will take up the majority of the screen real-estate. This will consist of images and pins from top users, boards and brands. It will also include content from anyone that you might have already started following.

Underneath the images are tags which work a lot like tags in Twitter or other social media sites. You can also see the comments that were added by whoever initially uploaded the image and you can see the person you know who pinned it (or it might say that it was 'picked for you' based on your interests).

From here, you can simply hover your mouse over any images that you want to find out more about and you'll see an option to 'like', to 'pin' or to send. If you click the image itself, it will become full screen and you'll see the board it came from along the right, as well as more pins from the website that it was found on.

Underneath, you also have the option to add your own comment, which may be a response to the comment that's already there and to browse other related pins.

That's already a lot to take on board (no pun intended)! As you can see, Pinterest has a little more of a steep learning curve as compared with other similar social media sites.

If you want to find pins of a particular subject matter, then your best bet is to head to the 'search' bar at the top left of the homepage. In here, you can now search for whatever it is you're trying to find. There are a *lot* of pins on here, so don't be afraid to type something specific.

You can also click the option on the right in order to see a list of popular tags and categories which will help to filter the items you're seeing.

Likewise, you can also click on the names of boards or users as you're browsing and this will take you to their collections. This is often how you discover the really great stuff

- it's just a matter of trying to find someone with similar interests and tastes to you, in which case you will land upon all the research and browsing they've done which you can then use in your own projects.

Next to the search bar is a button with your name on it and a red pin. If you click this, you'll be taken to your collection of boards. Your name will be along the top, next to a picture of a pin. Now you can use the tabs along the top to view all your boards, all your pins, all your likes, all your followers or everyone that *you* are following.

When you view your boards, you'll see that one of the options is a 'plus' sign with the option to create a new board. Likewise, when looking at your boards, you'll see the option to 'Add a Pin'. Creating a board of course allows you to add a new board which will be empty, while adding a pin lets you add new pins to your board. You can then enter the URL of an image you like, or a web page with lots of images you like, or you can upload something from your computer.

This is one way to populate your boards with relevant pins and will likely be the main method you use if you're a content creator. It's hard to build a brand with entirely content that you borrowed and didn't create.

On the other ahnd though, if you want to add pins in the *quickest* way possible, you'll find that the best way to do that is to just browse the boards of other users and then just click to repin their items to your own boards.

Above your collection of boards and pins, you'll also see a button that gives you the option to edit your profile. Click here and you'll be given the option to fill in some details about yourself.

Specifically the options you're given are:

- Name
- Picture
- Username
- About
- Location
- Website

Make sure that you use a picture that will grab the eye and look appealing and that your username matches your company's branding. Note that this will also become your URL, so if your username is 'NewTech' then your page will be pinterest.com/newtech.

You can also add your website here. Make sure that you do this and at the same time go ahead and confirm your website by adding a small bit of code to your page.

Spend some time on this page and make sure that you edit your profile to reflect well on your brand. This means that you should have a compelling 'about' section that explains what you do and tells people why they should be following you. Likewise, you should have a great profile image that will jump out and grab attention and that will match your branding.

If you click 'settings' meanwhile, you'll be given a few more extra options for personalizing your account and controlling its behaviour. This section allows you to set your gender, to choose whether you want your profile to be searchable through Google (you definitely do), how you want to receive notifications and whether you want to connect with your other social accounts.

YOUR STRATEGY

At this point, you now have a full understanding of how Pinterest works and you're set up with an account that looks the part and that should help more people to start finding the content you're creating.

Now all that's left is to actually *begin* marketing.

We've looked over most of the advantages of marketing on Pinterest already and we've seen how it lends itself well to promoting a website, blog or business. But now it's time to move away from the hypothetical and to start creating a business model that works.

Let's start with the basics. By looking at what makes *any* type of marketing strategy and any type of business successful.

And the single answer here is *value*. If you want to engage your audience, if you want to build customers and fans and if you want to engender loyalty, then you need to be offering high quality *value* to achieve all those things.

That means in other words, that you need to give people a concrete reason to want to spend time engaging with your brand.

The mistake that a lot of companies and marketers make on social media is simply to try and use it as a platform for promoting a product. They want to get direct sales, immediately and they're trying to reach a broader audience by doing this through social media.

You'll see this when you follow a company on Twitter that does nothing but talk about its products or services:

"Try out our latest products today!"

"Want to save time in the office? Our productivity tools are just for you!" "Hurry while stocks last!"

The equivalent on Pinterest is simply to post images from articles with no rhyme or reason, or to just post images of the same product over and over hoping someone will notice it.

This is unfortunately an entirely incorrect approach and social media just doesn't lend itself to that kind of promotion. Why? Because you need people to want to *follow* you on social media. And if all you're doing is posting about your company then you're really not going to give anyone a chance to do that. Would *you* follow a social media profile that only ever tried to sell its products to you? Or would you quickly get bored and unsubscribe?

Instead, you need to think like the top brands on Pinterest and offer the kind of service that people are looking for on the platform: inspiration, ideas and lifehacks.

The ideal type of company for Pinterest is a company that sells wedding decorations, or perhaps that prints wedding invitations. You can then create a Pinterest board that will share images of wedding decorations – both involving your own products and using other products. Make sure that the ideas are unique and interesting, that they provide style and elegance on a budget and that they offer the kinds of ideas that your followers might not have come up with themselves. This way, you give them an actual reason to follow you – because they're learning!

Likewise, you might create a Pinterest board about 'battlestations' if you sell computer parts. Battlestations are essentially PC set-ups for gamers that are designed to look cool with lots of glowing parts and large dual monitor set-ups.

Sell cupboards? Then you could create a board about organizational life hacks. Sell cooking ingredients? Then share pins of great meals and desserts and discuss the ingredients and the procedure in the comments underneath.

In any of these cases, you're giving people a reason to follow you on Pinterest because you're offering value in the form of ideas, inspiration or just aesthetic beauty.

If you're selling a physical product and especially something that looks beautiful or that has a 'chic' appeal, then you'll find that Pinterest is the perfect fit for your business.

But what if you sell insurance? What if you sell eBooks about making money through day trading? What if your niche isn't something that appeals to hipsters? How do you make this work on Pinterest?

The answer is that you need to go a little bit deeper and think about 'lifestyle' and about 'value proposition'.

In terms of lifestyle, it's pertinent to consider that every product or service that you sell, will ultimately support some kind of lifestyle and will appeal to a certain type of person. Fitness eBooks for instance appeal to people who like working out and who want to be in better shape. The 'fitness lifestyle' is an inspiring and visual concept that you can portray with pictures of people jogging on the beach listening to an MP3 player, or with pictures of people working out outdoors.

Likewise, if you sell holiday insurance, then the lifestyle is the 'travelling' lifestyle. You can post images of beautiful foreign destinations, or you can have boards outlining things to do in particular places.

'Value proposition' meanwhile refers to the value that your product or service *really* offers beyond the sum of its parts. The old saying goes that you 'don't sell hats, you sell warm heads'. What this means, is that the true *value* of the hat is in its ability to keep your head warm.

So if you can't post pictures of your 'hat' then you can always post pictures of your 'warm head'.

What is the value proposition of life insurance? Simple: it's keeping your family happy and safe after you're gone and it's looking after finances. As such then, your board doesn't need to include images of life insurance policies (the hat) but instead should include pictures of happy families enjoying days out together and doing fun things (the warm head). Your board could just be designed to give people that 'warm fuzzy feeling' by showing people having a great time, or it could be used to provide tips and ideas: how about ideas for things for people to do together as a family on a budget. Maybe it could be filled with pictures that humorously satirize the nature of the modern family?

Likewise, if your blog is about SEO and digital marketing, then your value proposition is business success, wealth and the feeling of accomplishment that comes from making it big online. Perhaps it's also the freedom that you gain when you work for yourself and aren't restrained to work in an office with a boss leaning over your shoulder. To demonstrate this in a

Pinterest board, you could show images of people working in exciting locations like huge libraries, or on the beach in a hammock. Likewise, you could show people in suits looking successful and well-dressed thanks to the money they managed to earn online.

The key either way here, is to come up with themes for your boards that deliver real value and purpose for Pinterest users while remaining 'on topic'. Don't just randomly repin pictures that vaguely relate, don't just promote your products and don't just post your articles randomly. If you do that you won't be providing value and you won't grow your viewership.

Think of your Pinterest profile almost like a service or a product in itself. The ideal scenario is that people will end up looking forward to checking out your pins or that they may even become reliant on your boards. They should be disappointed if ever your board gets taken down and the board should almost be able to exist on its own, as a separate entity from your business.

Selling Through Your Images

This still leaves us with one problem though.

If your board is about great interior design ideas and your company sells furniture and decorative items, then it's going to be very easy for you to include images of your products that people can click through to buy.

But if you sell life insurance and your board is about 'fun family days out' then you still won't be able to easily sell directly through the board. So how do you make sales from that?

On the whole, your objective here is not going to be to sell directly. Instead, the aim will be to raise awareness for your brand and to build trust and authority. The hope is that your audience will come to think of you as an expert on the subject of families and life insurance and as such, they will follow your links when they *do* want to find out more about getting a policy. This of course is not as direct a way to sell but in the long term it can actually be a lot more effective as you're building a long-term relationship and as you're establishing yourself as a thought leader in your field.

At the same time, you need to think about the comments that you're adding to your pictures. This is your opportunity to directly link the image back to your site and to promote your product. For instance, if you're uploading images of people doing home workouts to provide inspiration and ideas to your followers, then you can sell through those images by adding a note at the bottom explaining that they can find more similar moves in your eBook at THIS link.

The great thing about Pinterest is that it really does leverage the viral power of social networks. If your board is really delivering great value then this fact alone will be enough to ensure that it grows naturally. People will repin your pins, they will comment and they will discover what you're posting through the search button. If you're offering new content, if you're staying on topic and if you're providing real value by offering a genuine service of some kind, then people will gradually gravitate towards your brand and you'll build your following.

But that is not to say that there aren't also other things you can do to further accelerate your progress. Here are some of the ways you can grow your following more quickly:

Post Regularly: The more regularly you post, the more often your images will be found in searches. At the same time, they'll also come up in homefeeds more often, which means other users will be more likely to repin them and thereby share them with their audiences giving you more exposure.

Choose Your Tags Careful: As on Twitter, choosing the right hashtags is one of the most important ingredients when it comes to gaining maximum exposure for your images. The tags will dictate which searches bring up your images and this means that they'll be directly responsible for the number of people finding your brand.

When choosing your tags, make sure that you think about the types of things that commonly get searched for on the platform. Remember the kinds of things people use Pinterest for and remember that the audience is 85% female. Remember too that people are looking for images. 'How to' isn't as applicable here ('life hack' is a more suitable string).

Write Comments: If you upload an image without any comment then you give it no context. This means you won't be getting the very most from it, simply because people won't know what you're trying to say with the image. If it's a bodyweight exercise then explain how to do the exercise! If it's a decoration for the home, then explain how people can use it, what it's made from and where it can be bought. Make sure to link your brand to the image, otherwise people might just appreciate the image but never engage with your profile as the person who uploaded it!

Interact With Others: On social media, reciprocity is a very underrated tool. This is still a social network and therefore, it should be used as a communication tool. The more you talk to people, the more likely they will be to check out your profile and to look at your boards. So make sure that you're interacting, following, repining and more. If nothing else, this helps to build good will as you'll be helping those users to promote themselves too!

Integrate Your Website: One of the most important ways for you to spread your brand across Pinterest and to get found by more people is to properly link your website and your Pinterest account. There are a few ways that you should do this. One is by adding a link on your homepage to your Pinterest account. This way, someone who lands on your website for the first time and decides that they like your content, can decide that they want to follow you on social media as well and can then decide to check out your Pinterest and follow your account or your boards.

Another tip is to use 'Shareabolic' or a similar social sharing tool on your website. If you have a WordPress site, then these can be installed very easily and they will then allow people to quickly and easily 'Pin' an article that they found interesting along with an image. This then means there will be more people sharing your images and you'll gain more exposure as a result.

Cross Pollinate: You should also make sure that you occasionally try to cross pollinate between your social media channels. If you have a very successful Twitter account for instance, then occasionally tweet about the 'inspiring boards' you're creating at Pinterest. Likewise, you can share your pins to Facebook for people to see. Do this occasionally to help grow all of your accounts at once.

Think About Pinterest When You Create Content: If you've heard of 'clickbait' then you'll know how a lot of website owners are now creating content specifically to encourage shares on Facebook. This is content that uses an obtuse title in order to make people curious and to encourage more clicks as a result. It's frustrating but it works and sites like Buzzfeed have built their business off the back of it.

So the point is, that thinking about how you're going to share you content before you create it is a good move. The same goes for marketing on Pinterest.

If you're going to make an article successful on Pinterest then what does it need? Simple: it needs a great image that will make the article more compelling (this will also help when other people share your images and your pages). Make sure that you are creating unique images for your site and that they're designed in such a way as to really sell the content of your article or blog post and to encourage people to follow the URL. Some things that can work well are tips that can be portrayed *through* a single image, memes or inspirational quotes. Note as well that certain images automatically attract more attention than others – we are psychologically hardwired for instance to notice pictures of faces!
38

ADVANCED TECHNIQUES

The above is the basic approach that you should be taking to your Pinterest marketing and it explains how you're going to go about providing value on a regular basis and growing your audience.

But if you want to step up your game, then you should look at using some of the advanced tools that Pinterest offers. Compared to other social media sites, the amount of tools and support that Pinterest offers specifically for businesses and marketers is really quite staggering, so it's crucial that you start taking full advantage of this.

To get started with your business account, you need to visit this link:

https://business.pinterest.com.

If you don't already have a Pinterest account, then you just click 'Join as a Business' to get set up with your own business account.

If you *do* already have a Pinterest account, then thankfully there is the option to 'Convert Now' which lets you change your current account into a business account. This is completely free and takes a matter of seconds, so it's worth doing (see above for more reasons why).

From here, you can then install a Pin It button easily to your page, your can get a 'Follow Me' button to add to your website too, or you can set up your analytics.

Using analytics is an incredibly good idea, because it will allow you to see which of your articles and images are being shared on Pinterest and being interacted with. This is a hugely useful tool for assessing which of your content is performing the best and that helps you to refine your approach. Maybe your memes are getting the most shares? Maybe shorter articles perform better? Looking at these metrics let you know. This is a very powerful feature that a lot of other social sites just can't come close to!

We discussed the use of 'rich article pins' earlier but in fact there are actually *six* types of rich pins. These include:

- App
- Movie
- Recipe
- Article
- Product
- Place

That means that you can provide additional information about your pin and set up your site so that when someone else shares your pin, the additional information will be there automatically.

Go to this link: https://developers.pinterest.com/docs/rich-pins/overview/ to apply for rich pins via the 'validator'. From there, you then simply need to add some meta information to your website so that Pinterest can see what type of content you've shared.

Note: If you want to prevent your pages from showing as rich pins, you simply add the following line to the head section of your HTML:

```
<meta name="pinterest-rich-pin" content="false" />
```

There's also some code you can use to prevent your content from appearing as pins at all. This however is not a particularly useful tool for a marketer!

For marketers, one of the most interesting types of pin *other* than the rich article pin, is the product pin. A product pin essentially enables you to show availability for an item and to show the pricing in real time. If you don't have the 'Buy' button on your pin, this is the next best thing for making it easy for people to buy your products and to learn more about them.

Again, you need meta content for this to work. This time the following markup:

```
<meta property="og:title" content="Name of your product" />
<meta property="og:type" content="product" />
<meta property="og:price:amount" content="1.00" />
<meta property="og:price:currency" content="USD" />
```

Pinterest has some useful utility for influencer marketing, thanks to its own 'Pinterest Email' feature, which was introduced in May 2013. This tool allows you to send your contacts on Pinterest a personalized message that might recommend a specific pin, or which can be used to open up a dialogue.

What makes this useful is that it means you can now get in touch with other users that are performing well on the site. In turn, this then means you can invite them to work together, or

42

can suggest particular partnerships. This can be beneficial for both brands and if you gradually approach more and more highly influential users, you can progress up the ladder to increase your rich.

You can also use this to turn prospects into buyers – send someone who is engaging with your content a pin that you think they'll like, or that you think will solve an issue they're having, and it could turn into a sale for you, or at least a new subscriber or follower!

If you want to go one step further with your website/Pinterest integration, then you should look into adding widgets. You can get widgets for both your Pinterest page *and* for your boards specifically. Either of these can then be added to the sidebar of your website, which will make your profile much more tempting for people to follow. Not only will your visitors be able to see that you're *on* Pinterest but this way they'll also be able to see the type of content you're sharing and the kind of value you're offering. This is also a great way to ensure that your website stays looking active if you're busy and don't have time to add new blog posts for instance.

As we mentioned previously, Pinterest is the perfect platform for launching a competition. The visual nature of Pinterest creates a fun opportunity for people to send in their ideas for interior design, or novel uses for your products. Likewise, you can run contests where you award the most inspiring boards on the platform that solve a particular problem that you posit.

Either way, this is a great way to get more people engaging with your brand which can in turn also lead to more of your pins getting shared throughout social networks.

When running contests though, make sure that you adhere to the guidelines that Pinterest sets out for brands. You can find these here:

https://business.pinterest.com/en- gb/brand-guidelines.

If you want to make your marketing strategy even *more* advanced then you should look at the ways you can leverage other tools and software to streamline your workflow. As we'll see, utilizing the right apps and services can save you a lot of time and help you to get more work done more quickly.

Here are some of the best ones to consider using... (IFTTT.com)

IFTTT is an absolutely incredible tool that allows you to synchronize a large number of different apps and services that you use on the web. It works by letting you set up certain actions on social media, web apps or even WordPress to work as 'triggers'. These triggers can then *cause* an action on a range of other connected services.

The most basic example of this would be to have your WordPress page automatically share posts to Pinterest when you upload them. Make sure you're adding in the rich articles metatags, and then let IFTTT take care of the rest by adding the articles to the pages automatically. This can save you a lot of time but do remember that you don't want to make *all* your content automatically added – you also need to actively select some of your Pinterest content to make sure that you're providing value.

There are also a ton of other 'recipes' (as they're known on the site) that you can create through IFTTT to streamline your Pinterest posting. For instance, why not have your Instagram pictures automatically shared to Pinterest as well? Or how about the Instagram pictures that you like? Alternatively you can go the other tact and make sure that your Twitter followers are notified each time you add new content to Pinterest. Now, each new pin you add is another opportunity for your followers to gravitate toward your Pinterest account and increase the number of followers you have there.

You can sync this up with any of your social media accounts which will help to keep your profile looking busy!

There is a Pinterest Chrome plugin that can save you a huge amount of time on Pinterest yet again. What this allows you to do is to easily share any image you come across online (as long as you're using the Chrome browser) by just hovering your mouse over it. This is much faster than having to navigate to Pinterest each time you want to add a photo and then manually enter the URL and it basically means you're more likely to add more high quality content as you find it to your account.

Pinterest also has great apps for Android and iOS – both of which make it even easier for you to manage your account and to add new photos or respond to comments. The great thing about the apps is that you can use them wherever you are, which will again save you time and which means you can promote your brand when it's convenient for you instead of having it eat into your other business activities.

The other great thing about the app is that if you hit the 'plus' sign in the top left, you can quickly take photos that you can then add as pins. If you have a personal brand, or if you want to show off your company hard at work in the office, then this is a great tool! Other than this additional feature, using the Pinterest app is broadly similar to navigating the website, so you should find it very intuitive.

HOW BUSINESSES USE PINTEREST

If you're still reading then congratulations, you now know Pinterest marketing inside out and should be ready to start achieving great things through the app.

But if you're still feeling anxious about diving in, it might help you to see some examples of other brands that have managed to succeed. These companies have largely used the exact same techniques that we've discussed – delivering *value* to their audience and then linking it back to the products and services they sell. Here are some great examples of top brands and how they've worked their magic...

Etsy

Etsy is pretty much the 'eBay of crafts' and allows its users to sell all kinds of things they've made (of course the company takes a small cut). Common products to find on Etsy include handmade jewellery, paintings, ornaments and more.

As you can imagine then, this is a perfect example of a creative and 'visual' brand that is ideally suited to Pinterest.

And Etsy has made sure to take *full* advantage of that fit. They have boards focussing on everything from interior design, to pets, to gardening, to cooking. With well over 460,000 followers, their boards are doing very well and they even allow viewers to easily buy the items that they like the looks of.

Swarovski

Swarovski has one board in particular that does very well on Pinterest, which is its 'Wedded Bliss' board. This board has over 1,500,000 followers and growing. The board works well because it really focusses on the *emotions* involved in getting married (hence 'bliss') and because it provides useful inspiration for those getting married. At the same time, it relates to their products without being an obviously promotional subject.

Mashable

Mashable is a great example of a blog that is doing well on Pinterest. With over 1,500,000 followers, the company works by focussing on the most visually appealing aspects of technology: such as infographics, apps and products.

HTC One

HTC One is doing a great job with marketing in general and has set itself apart as a very 'trendy' mobile phone manufacturer. Pinterest only helps it to cement this impression, where the company has been running contests. A simple promotion 'repin to win your very own HTC one' was enough to gain over 3,700 comments and even more repins. The contest was actually a partnership with a leading social media authority already doing well on the site, which nicely rolls two very potent marketing strategies into one highly effective approach.

L.L. Bean

L.L. Bean has more followers than any other brand currently on Pinterest: that's over 5,300,000! They showcase all kinds of outdoors activities, again focussing on the lifestyle that surrounds their products. People want to fill their home-feeds with imagery that's aesthetically appealing and that makes them feel good when they look at it – so keep this in mind as you populate your own boards!

As you can see, all these big brands are using Pinterest in precisely the way we've outlined: to share content that people will enjoy viewing and that will promote the lifestyle and value proposition of their products. Good marketing doesn't have to be 'on the nose' – look for ways to get people excited about your brand and to help them feel inspired and to come up with ideas. If you can do those things, then your boards will succeed.

YOUR PINTEREST PLAN

Now you have all the pieces, it's time to put them together to form a plan that you can follow one step at a time in order to build your viewers and to gain mass influence.

Step 1: Build Your Brand

The first step is to build your brand. This means you need to make sure that you know 'who you are' as a business before you tackle Pinterest.

This is something that should come before you begin on *any* social media site. You need to make sure you have a clear 'mission statement' that ties all your different products, blog posts and activities together. This should then be expressed through a logo which should bleed through into your web design. Make sure you have a website set up that has a design language consistent with the rest of your branding and then bring that same color scheme and logo to each of the social media sites you sign up with.

It's this consistency that will ultimately ensure that *each* interaction with a customer increases your brand visibility and helps to build your authority. This will also considerably help you to appear more professional as you maintain the same design sensibilities in everything you do, rather than appearing not to have any particular strategy. The mantra of most businesses when it comes to social media marketing is to 'be everywhere' and consistency is key with that.

Make sure your Pinterest account is a *business* account and link it with your website using the code that Pinterest gives you.

Step 2: Link Your Accounts

Now you should do a little prep work to make sure that your work flow is going to be as smooth as possible and to help yourself more easily add new content to your Pinterest boards/share users between your accounts.

Make sure that you have a link to your Pinterest page right on your homepage then and even consider adding a widget in your sidebar so that your visitors can migrate to Pinterest from there. Likewise, ensure that you Tweet about your Pinterest page and that you share your Instagram images on Pinterest. You can use IFTTT to set up some of these relationships and that will save you a lot of time. You should also install the Instagram app on your mobile device and the Instagram plugin for Chrome – both of which will make it easier for you to keep adding new content.

Use Shareaholic meanwhile to add social sharing buttons to your website, thereby allowing other people to share your content. This is also a good time to set-up rich article pins with your website so that the pins that *do* get shared from your website will have titles and information under them.

Step 3: Provide Value

Now begins the most important part of your Pinterest marketing strategy: delivering value. Make sure that you are posting content to Pinterest regularly and that you have come up with some kind of 'angle' for your boards that will really appeal to your audience. You might focus on inspirational images, beautiful images, or tips and ideas. Either way, your board should fulfil some kind of purpose and be useful to your followers. It should be so valuable as to essentially stand as its own 'product' and attract viewers on its own merit. Only occasionally will you then link your images back to products you're selling, or try to get people to sign up to your mailing list etc.

Make sure to carefully choose the tags you add to your pins so that people can find your images and write comments underneath to provide context. Good titles can also help a lot. If you're still unsure of what works, then spend some time looking at the boards we recommended to get ideas.

You should also make sure to keep posting great value content to your website that people can share through Pinterest. Use analytics to see which content is performing best and make sure that you feature attractive images that will grab attention and get people to pin and repin.

You should also spend some time interacting with the community and building relationships: that means repining the content you find from other users, posting comments and sending messages to your followers. This will help you to build more of a relationship with those users.

Step 4: Monetize

Monetization is the step that should come last, but of course it's still very important. The best way to monetize your

Pinterest account is to add your own products or to mention your services in the text below your posts. The great thing about selling products through Pinterest is that the new 'Buy Now' button will allow you to sell directly like an eCommerce store. Otherwise, use the 'Rich Product' pins and use these to keep your viewers updated regarding the items you have in stock, the price and where they can get hold of them.

More important than these direct sales though is just to build your audience and to gain their trust so that you can bring them to your website when they're *looking* for services and products like yours. This is when social media is its most effective, so don't get impatient and drive them away!

FINAL WORDS

There you have it: that's everything you could possibly need to know to start succeeding on Pinterest!

Really though, the most important learning will occur 'on the job' as you go through the act of posting content and using the tool. When you first sign up, it might seem like a complicated platform to begin with, but you'll quickly find your footing and at that point it can be a lot of fun too.

As some final advice, consider the following 'dos and don'ts' to guide you through…

DO Make sure that all your content is offering real value for your followers.

DO Add useful descriptions to anything you upload.

DO Pick the right tags!

DON'T Just try to sell products!

DO Set up useful 'automated' systems to save you time.

DON'T Rely on these though, or you'll end up with a lot of random content.

DO Think about how articles you write for your blog post will work on Pinterest.

DON'T Post irregularly and leave your account looking barren.

DON'T Just rely on repining – add your own unique content!

DO Upgrade to a business account.

DO Verify your website so that you can see analytics.

DO Include social sharing buttons on your content.

DON'T Think that Pinterest is less important than other social media sites!

And while we're at it, let's consider some cool ideas for things you can do with Pinterest, which will hopefully leave you with a bit of inspiration before you get started.

Designing Your Website or Logo

A great way to get to grips with Pinterest is to try using it yourself *not* as a marketer. When designing your website or logo, you can use a Pinterest board to collect images that you like the looks of and that you think should inspire the artistic direction you're going to go with. You'll find this really helps you to bring everything together into a cohesive design at the end and this understanding will prove useful when you're trying to appeal to other users with your own content.

Bodyweight Exercises

If you have a fitness blog, then using it to share bodyweight exercises is a great idea. This is the kind of thing that allows you to provide genuinely useful tips but through just a single image and some text!

Eye Candy

Some people love staring at pictures of beautiful holiday locations, other people love looking at stunning cars. Sometimes creating a board that's all about making us salivate is a great way to get fans – and as you're building up the desire factor, it will be great when it comes to selling!

Life Hacks

People love lifehacks and actually Pinterest is one of the big reasons for this! Try posting tips that you can convey in a single image. Life hacks can also be applied to pretty much any niche whether it's 'gardening' life hacks or tidying life hacks!

Motivation

Motivational posters are popular online and can apply to a range of different topics. Why not create a board that focusses on motivational images and text relating to your niche or industry?

Those are just a few ideas but the possibilities are endless so dive in and start experimenting! Good luck and happy pinning!

Printed by Libri Plureos GmbH in Hamburg,
Germany